GIFT
WRAPPING
WITH
TEXTILES

GIFT WRAPPING
WITH TEXTILES

Stylish Ideas from Japan

CHIZUKO MORITA

PHOTOGRAPHS BY Shuichi Yamagata

TRANSLATED BY Kirsten McIvor

KODANSHA INTERNATIONAL
Tokyo • New York • London

CONTENTS

A Wrap for All Seasons   28

Four-Petal Wrap   29

Twin-Knot Wrap   29

Rabbit Wrap #1   32

Rabbit Wrap #2   32

Goldfish Wrap   33

Bouncing Ball   36

Cookie Wrap   36

Long-Tailed Pheasant   37

Wrapping Books   40

Wrapping CDs   40

Rectangular Wrap   41

Simple Flower Wrap   44

Carnation Wrap   44

Falling Cherry Blossoms   45

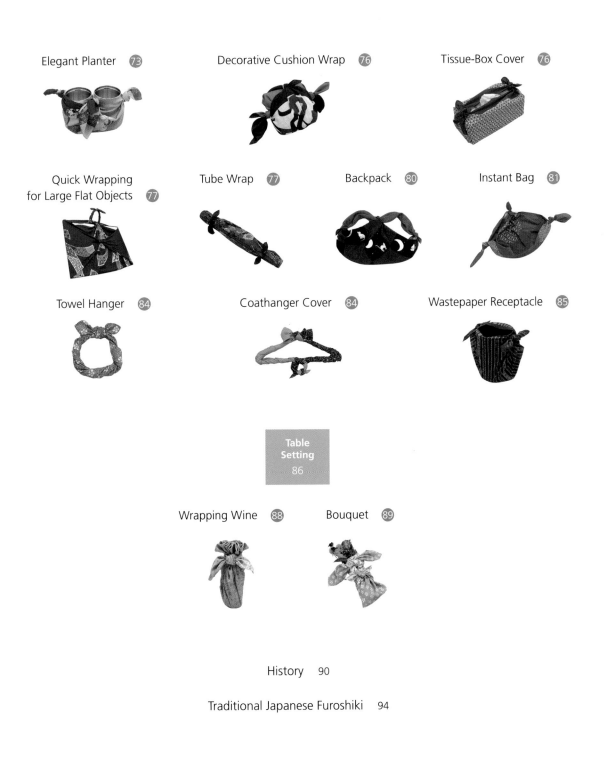

Distributed in the United States by Kodansha America, LLC, and in the
United Kingdom and continental Europe by Kodansha Europe Ltd.

Published by Kodansha International Ltd., 17–14 Otowa 1-chome,
Bunkyo-ku, Tokyo 112–8652.

Copyright © 2005 by Chizuko Morita.
Photographs copyright © 2005 by Shuichi Yamagata.
All rights reserved. Printed in Japan.
ISBN 978–4–7700–2736–8

First edition, 2005
18 17 16 15 14 13 12 11 10 09   12 11 10 9 8 7 6 5 4

Library of Congress Cataloging-in-Publication Data

Morita, Chizuko
  Gift wrapping with textiles: stylish ideas from Japan/
  Chizuko Morita; photographs by Shuichi Yamagata;
  translated by Kirsten McIvor.

  1. Textile crafts. 2. Fukusa. 3. Gift wrapping.
  4. Wrapping cloths—Japan. I. Title.

  TT699.M67 2006   746—dc22   2005044561

www.kodansha-intl.com

INTRODUCTION

Be it wine, books, or home-made cookies, there is something immensely satisfying about wrapping a gift in cloth. But just why is this?

Because textiles let us give free rein to our imagination. A piece of cloth is thin, soft, and flat. It has no shape of its own. Only when wrapped around something does it take on three-dimensional form: a new shape, created by our own hands.

Using cloth, you can wrap just about anything of any shape or size. Whether it be square, spherical, cube-shaped, oblong, or oval, few activities offer greater delight than finding ingenious and creative ways to wrap something attractively, taking your inspiration from the item itself. Watch as your creation takes shape before your eyes, in virtually no time at all, and with minimal fuss.

To run your fingers over a piece of fabric with its soft sensual texture and extraordinarily beautiful colors and patterns is curiously soothing. It is something I often do when stressed or tired, and when I do, my worries and fatigue seem to melt away. Does the cloth somehow absorb them all?

And wrapping in textiles is not just fun for you; a gift presented in an attractive fabric is guaranteed to delight and surprise the recipient. Wrapping an object is like dressing it in a costume; this provides a marvelous opportunity to impress others with your sense of style. Use it to project an image that matches your mood and the occasion—chic and understated, intricate and ornate, festive and brightly colored.

The Japanese have an everyday cloth called a *furoshiki* that has been used, since ancient times, for many different purposes, including for wrapping a gift, covering an object to be carried, or as a decorative wall hanging. The furoshiki used for gift-wrapping have always occupied a special place in traditional Japanese customs and etiquette, particularly on occasions such as weddings.

That said, the modernization of Japan's lifestyle means that furoshiki are no longer used as much as they were.

It struck me one day that it would be a shame to allow the beautiful furoshiki, with its traditional colors and patterns, to disappear along with the culture of wrapping and presenting gifts in cloth. Surely there were ways to utilize these beautiful textiles in our daily life?

This was about thirteen years ago, and my answer was to learn all I could from our predecessors, then add my own creative touches and ideas to devise new ways of wrapping in cloth, as well as create new purposes for wrapping.

This book presents the most popular of those ideas, in addition to ways to decorate your home for different occasions, again using textiles. All are simple, fascinating, and fun.

I hope they will inspire you to take up a bandanna or handkerchief, or any favorite piece of cloth on hand, and have fun using it to wrap a gift or add a decorative touch to your home that makes a statement about your personality and sense of style.

And if you ever have the chance to visit Japan, or obtain furoshiki cloths by some other means, such as over the Internet, I hope you will take the opportunity to enjoy the special pleasure of wrapping with furoshiki, and experience for yourself a unique facet of Japanese culture.

Chizuko Morita

BEFORE YOU START

THE ENJOYMENT AND ADVANTAGES OF WRAPPING WITH TEXTILES

■ Soft texture—Whether supple silk, crisp cotton, or slippery synthetic, textiles are soft to the touch, and soothing to the soul.

■ Creates a costume—Sometimes sharp lines, sometimes soft. Wrap an object in cloth and you create for it a costume that adds character, and shows off its shape to advantage.

■ Can be redone any number of times—Unlike wrapping paper, cloth wraps can be used again and again. Even if you get it wrong the first time, relax, and try again.

■ Environment friendly—The importance of this cannot be understated. Cloth can be used over and over: unwrap, and use it to wrap something else.

■ Lets you give the joy of wrapping—When you wrap something in cloth, the person unwrapping it is left with that single piece of fabric, which can form part of the gift. Not only is it fun to choose material to match the gift, but, when you hand someone a gift wrapped in cloth, you are also showing just how satisfying wrapping in cloth can be.

SELECTING A CLOTH

What Makes a Good Wrapping Cloth

First of all, there are some basic but vital things to learn if you want to wrap attractively using textiles. Think about the size of the cloth and what you will wrap. If the cloth is too big, it will be baggy; too small and the contents will protrude. Choosing a cloth to match the size of the object is an important part of making your wrapping neat and attractive. As a guide, when wrapping a square box for example, the box should be around one-third the length of a line drawn across the cloth from corner to corner.

A NOTE ABOUT FUROSHIKI

The cloths come in various sizes, for different purposes. Furoshiki are produced in about eight standard sizes, the smallest measuring 18 inches (45 cm) square and the largest 96 inches (240 cm) square. Woven using a loom, furoshiki can be produced in sizes up to approximately 52 inches (130 cm) in width without seams.

Furoshiki with a traditional image or other picturelike motif have a definite top, bottom, left, and right. In others, the presence of a large motif in the bottom left corner indicates orientation. Most furoshiki are machine-stitched top and bottom, with selvedges on the left and right edges. Furoshiki range in price from a few dollars to as much as fifty dollars or more (depending on the design, size, and quality of the material), so select one according to usage (will you reuse it again?) and the recipient.

Size Chart

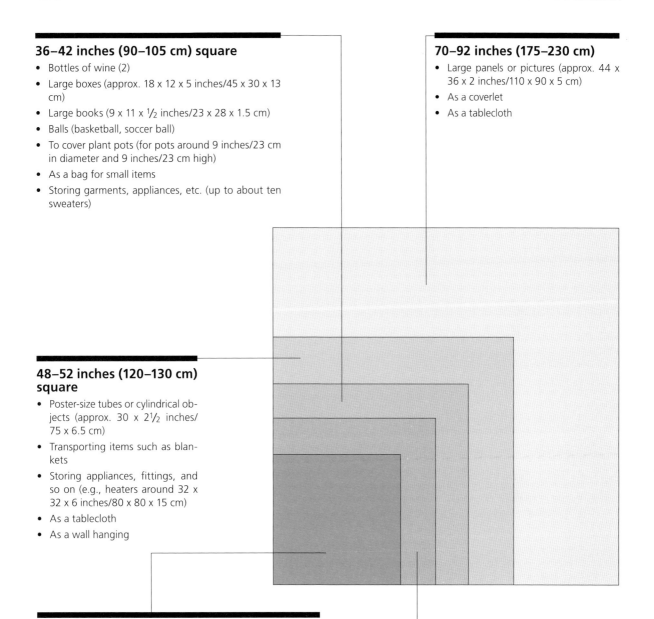

36–42 inches (90–105 cm) square

- Bottles of wine (2)
- Large boxes (approx. 18 x 12 x 5 inches/45 x 30 x 13 cm)
- Large books (9 x 11 x ½ inches/23 x 28 x 1.5 cm)
- Balls (basketball, soccer ball)
- To cover plant pots (for pots around 9 inches/23 cm in diameter and 9 inches/23 cm high)
- As a bag for small items
- Storing garments, appliances, etc. (up to about ten sweaters)

70–92 inches (175–230 cm)

- Large panels or pictures (approx. 44 x 36 x 2 inches/110 x 90 x 5 cm)
- As a coverlet
- As a tablecloth

48–52 inches (120–130 cm) square

- Poster-size tubes or cylindrical objects (approx. 30 x 2½ inches/ 75 x 6.5 cm)
- Transporting items such as blankets
- Storing appliances, fittings, and so on (e.g., heaters around 32 x 32 x 6 inches/80 x 80 x 15 cm)
- As a tablecloth
- As a wall hanging

18–24 inches (45–60 cm) square

- Small boxes of candy, cookies, and so on (approx. 5 x 5 x ½ inches/12 x 12 x 1.5 cm–8 x 6 x 1 inches/20 x 15 x 2 cm)
- Jewelry boxes (approx. 3 x 2½ x 1 inches/8 x 6 x 3 cm)
- Stationery, writing implements, pencil cases (approx. 7 x 2½ x 1 inches/18 x 6 x 3 cm)
- Books (four or so paperbacks, or one larger book approx. 7 x 10 inches/18 x 25 cm)
- CDs (1–4)
- Fruit the size of a large apple or grapefruit
- Balls (baseball, softball)
- Tissue boxes
- Small potted plants (7 inches/18 cm in diameter and 5 inches/12 cm high)

28–30 inches (70–75 cm) square

- Bottles of wine, champagne, whiskey, and so on
- Flowers (up to 10)
- Candy, cakes (boxes around 12 x 10 x 4 inches/30 x 25 x 10 cm)
- Books (5 x 8 x ½ inches/13 x 19 x 1.5 cm)
- Mufflers, scarves, T-shirts, and so on
- Plates (approx. 10 inches/25 cm in diameter)

TECHNIQUES

Tying Attractive Knots

• By tying a piece of fabric in different ways, you can create all sorts of gift wrapping designs, and even transform your cloth into a bag or backpack. Tie knots firmly. A loose knot that stretches may soon come undone.

• When you hold the ends of a cloth to knot them, pull the corners firmly. Pulling on parts of the cloth other than the corners will destroy the balance of the knot. The knot will also lose its strength, and may even come undone.

• Rather than tying small tight knots at the ends of the fabric, tie them a reasonable length back from the tip, so that a minimum of 1 1/2 inches (3–4 cm) protrudes from the knot.

The Three Basic Knots

Learn the three basic knots required to reproduce the wrapping designs in this book. Each is easily mastered.

Square Knot

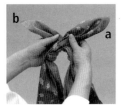    

1. Cross "a" over "b."

2. Entwine forming a half-knot.

3. Pull ends to lengthen in preparation for tying final half-knot.

4. Cross ends again and tie a second half-knot.

5. Pull "a" and "b" to left and right to tighten knot.

NOTE: One option for untying a square knot is to loosen it little by little. However for very tight square knots, an easier way to untie it is to pull the ends of the knotted fabric in opposite directions to raise the knot, then hold the knot with one hand, and pull on the cloth with the other.

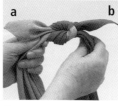  

1. Grab fabric firmly below knot.

2. Bring "a" over "b."

3. Wrap fingers around knot and slide knot to the right.

Single Knot

1. Hold one corner of the cloth and pull tight.

2. Make loop.

3. Pass corner through loop.

4. Pull tight.

Plain Knot

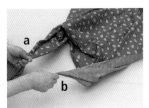

1. Hold a corner in each hand.

2. Cross "b" over "a."

3. Bring "b" under "a."

4. Loop "b" over "a," then . . .

5. . . . pass "b" through loop.

6. Pull "b" out and pull tight.

Pleating and Twisting

Pleats, Version 1

1. Decide where you want the pleats.

2. Gather cloth into pleats about 1½ inches (4 cm) wide.

3. Finish pleating and follow next instructions.

Pleats, Version 2

1. Hold corner of cloth up, and . . .

2. . . . with your other hand gather the cloth together at intervals of around ½ inch (1.5 cm).

Twisting   From the knot of a single knot

1. Hold cloth below knot with one hand, and fabric directly above the knot with the other.

2. Rotate cloth above knot around index or middle finger, twisting fabric while using your thumb for support.

3. Leave enough of the fabric untwisted to tie a knot.

CARING FOR TEXTILES

Iron out creases

Knotting fabric leaves creases, so iron it after untying.

Silk and synthetic fabrics: Place a cloth on top and press using medium heat setting. Do not use steam.

Cotton: Press without ironing cloth using a hot iron. Use starch for a crisper finish. Steam may be used.

Cleaning

Follow instructions on label to remove any stains or soiling.

Silk and synthetic fabrics: Use benzine or other recommended solvent on cotton wool to remove stains.

Cotton: For coloreds, use soap and wash by hand.

Putting away textiles

After use, fold textiles to store. Ensure soft fabrics such as silk keep their shape by folding around tissue paper and placing each individual piece of cloth in a paper bag. To store cotton and other fabrics neatly and ensure they retain their shape, place each piece of cloth on a cardboard backing to stack.

GIFT WRAPPING

Wrapping a gift is a way of expressing your gratitude or congratulations to the recipient. By taking the time and trouble to wrap your gift in a special way, you send a message that words cannot convey. The infinite creative possibilities of textiles mean you can choose a style of wrapping specifically to suit the recipient and the purpose.

A Wrap for All Seasons

This is the basic wrap for gifts in Japan, used for celebrations and a variety of other purposes. A simple knot with a loose corner draped over the edge combine for simple elegance. This style can be used for oval containers and various other shapes, as well as rectangular boxes. The key is to achieve the right balance between the size of the object and the size of the cloth.

TO WRAP
Box (approx. 12 x 9 x 3 inches/ 30 x 22 x 8 cm)

CLOTH
Piece of silk, approx. 28 inches (70 cm) square

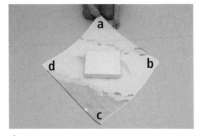

1. Spread cloth as a diamond and place box in center.

2. Pull "a" over the box and tuck underneath.

3. Pull "c" over box, leaving corner out.

4. Holding "b" in your left hand, gather surplus fabric in your right and bring "b" into the center, tidying the protrusions as you do.

5. Holding "d" in your right hand, gather surplus fabric in your left and bring "d" into the center.

6. Tie "b" and "d" in a firm square knot on top of the box. Adjust and tidy finished package as necessary.

Four-Petal Wrap

This is a lovely gift wrap for any square box. Selecting a fabric with varying colors will give the finished "flower" an added infusion of color.

TO WRAP
Square box (approx. 9 x 9 x 4 inches/23 x 23 x 10 cm)

CLOTH
Piece of silk, approx. 28 inches (70 cm) square

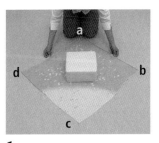

1. Spread cloth as a diamond and place box in center.

2. Tie "b" and "d" in a square knot.

3. Adjust corners.

4. Turn box and tie "a" and "c" in a firm square knot.

Twin-Knot Wrap

A little know-how and ingenuity is all it takes to wrap a long box beautifully. The trick is to use the surplus cloth at top and bottom to make up for the lack of cloth on left and right.

TO WRAP
Long, narrow box (approx. 18 x 5 x 4 inches/45 x 13 x 10 cm)

CLOTH
Piece of silk, approx. 28 inches (70 cm) square

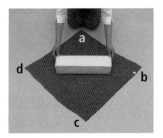

1. Spread cloth as a diamond and place box in center.

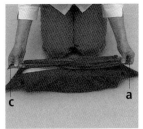

2. Bring "a" and "c" into center and cross with "a" toward "b" and "c" toward "d."

3. Tie "a" and "b" (not "c") in a firm square knot.

4. Tie "c" and "d" in a firm square knot.

Rabbit Wrap #1

The item you wish to wrap becomes the body of the rabbit. Perfect for gifts able to be rolled tightly such as mufflers, sweaters, and T-shirts. For added impact, choose a cloth that complements the color of the contents especially well.

TO WRAP
Muffler

CLOTH
Two pieces of cotton, 20 inches (50 cm) square

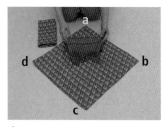

1. Spread one cloth as a diamond. Place the tightly rolled muffler on the cloth at the front.

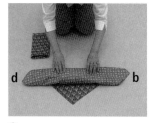

2. Roll up completely.

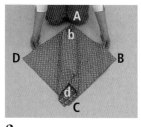

3. Lay the wrapped muffler vertically on the second cloth and wrap the second cloth around the muffler.

4. Bring "C" out from under "d," wrap it around "d," and tie them in a plain knot.

5. Adjust to make the rabbit: the knot becomes its face, and "d" and "C" become the ears.

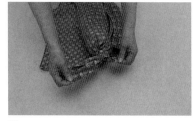

6. Tie "B" and "D" using a square knot.

7. Tie "b" and "A" using a plain knot to make the tail.

Rabbit Wrap #2

Here is a rabbit design almost too adorable to unwrap, with all the fun and satisfaction of making a doll. The key is to make the ears and tail pointy and alert. Either the front or back of the knot can form the face, whichever you prefer. When deciding back and front, consider the pattern on the fabric.

TO WRAP
One apple, ball, or other small round object

CLOTH
Piece of cotton, approx. 20 inches (50 cm) square

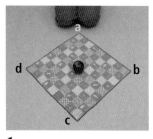

1. Spread cloth as a diamond and place apple in middle.

2. Gather corners "a" and "c" together over the apple, and . . .

3. . . . tie a single knot.

4. Separate and adjust the rabbit's ears.

5. Cross "b" and "d" behind.

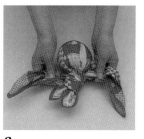

6. Bring both corners to front, and tie in a square knot to make tail.

7. Tidy to finish, adjusting ears and tail. Consider tucking in corner opposite tail if you find it distracts.

Goldfish Wrap

With his jaunty tail and fins, this fishy fellow will bring a smile to the face of any child (or indeed adult). Use a bag of candy or chocolates for the body, and note how the fabric is distributed cleverly to form the tail and fins.

TO WRAP
Bag of chocolates or other small gift measuring around 5 x 5 inches (13 x 13 cm)

CLOTH
Piece of cotton, approx. 20 inches (50 cm) square, preferably double sided

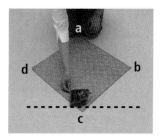

1. Spread the cloth in a diamond. Place the bag of chocolates around 1 inch (2.5 cm) below "c," to define what will become the dorsal fin.

2. From the position in step 1, roll the bag toward the opposite corner, them bring "a" up over it.

3. Roll up toward "c" . . .

4. . . . leaving about 1 inch (2.5 cm) for the dorsal fin. Fold "b" underneath.

5. Pull "b" toward "d."

6. Tie "d" and "b" in a single knot.

7. Open out "d" to display the back of the fabric, and make into the tail. Adjust dorsal fin "c" as well. Attach a button for the eye.

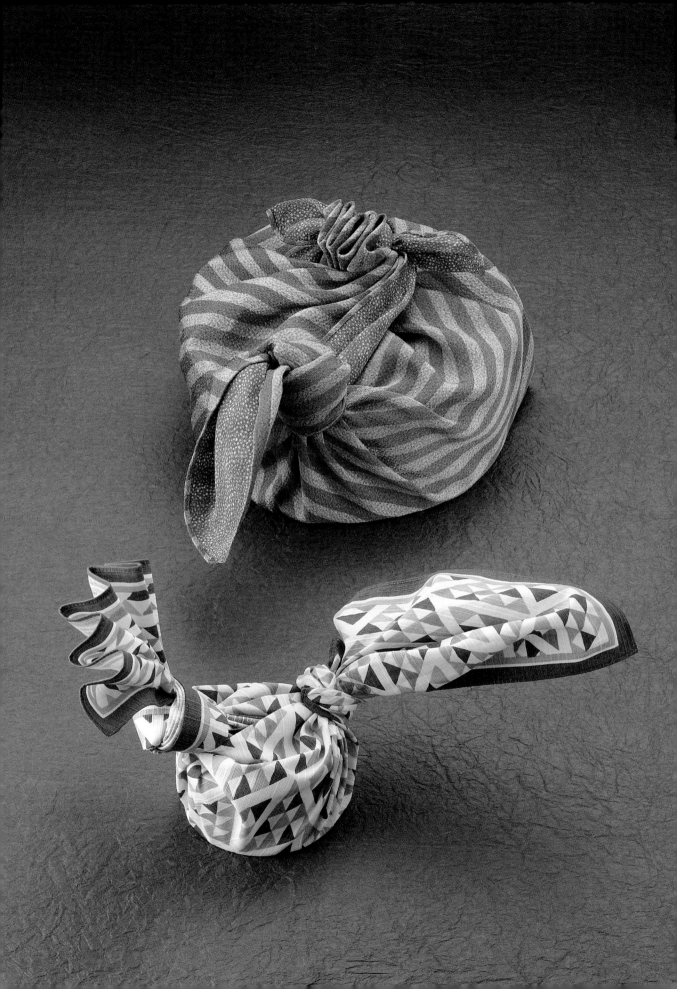

Bouncing Ball

The handle gives this design particular appeal. The trick is to achieve the right balance of handle, sphere, and knot. Perfect not only for balls, but also large melons for a party or picnic. Try wrapping softballs or other round objects.

TO WRAP
Basketball, soccer ball, volleyball, and so on

CLOTH
Piece of cotton, 42 inches (105 cm) square

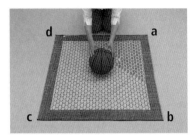

1. Spread cloth as a square, place ball in center.

2. Bring "a" and "d" together and tie in a square knot over the ball.

3. Pass "b" and "c" from back to front under knot, pulling fabric tightly to eliminate as much excess fabric as possible and accentuate the shape of the ball.

4. Twist "b" and "c" to form cordlike handle, leaving around 4 inches (10 cm) untwisted at the end of each. (See page 23 for instructions on twisting.)

5. Form a loop and tie the ends with a square knot.

Cookie Wrap

Use this wrapping technique for a can of cookies, candies, or other edibles. Fabric spilling over the top accentuates the curves of the round container. Make the gathers on top full and crisp, and wrap as if adding a tail. Perfect for oval containers.

TO WRAP
A medium-sized round container (approx. 8 inches/20 cm in diameter x 3 inches/8 cm high)

CLOTH
Piece of rayon crepe, approx. 28 inches (70 cm) square

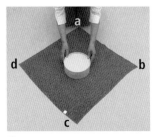

1. Spread cloth as a diamond and place container in center.

2. Fold "c" inward.

3. Bring fabric folded in step 2 to top of container.

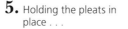

4. Make vertical pleats in this section measuring approximately 1½ inches (3–4 cm) wide. (See page 22 for instructions on how to form pleats.)

5. Holding the pleats in place . . .

6. . . . cross "d" over top, then . . .

7. . . . cross "b" over top in the opposite direction.

8. Tie "b" and "d" in a square knot behind pleats. Adjust knot.

9. Tie "a" at edge of container using a single knot for a draped effect.

Long-Tailed Pheasant

Give a dainty box of treats a whimsical look. For best results, make the pleats about 1 inch (2.5 cm) wide, tie a strong single knot, and pull firmly out to both sides.

TO WRAP
A small tin, box, or container (around 4 inches/10 cm in diameter x 1½ inches/4 cm high)

CLOTH
Piece of cotton, approx. 20 inches (50 cm) square

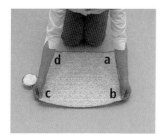

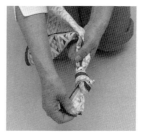

1. Spread cloth as a square.

2. Make pleats about 1 inch (2.5 cm) wide along edge from "b" to "c."

3. Fasten pleats using a single knot.

4. Place tin inside pleats, standing pleats up at the edge.

5. Tie "a" and "d" using a plain knot to form tail.

6. To finish, fan out pleats to form the feathered head.

Wrapping Books

In earlier days, Japanese students carried their books to school wrapped like this. You can lie them down, bundle them together, or stand them up. Achieving different looks from the same design just adds to the pleasure of wrapping in cloth. This will work for books of all sizes. You can gauge the size of the cloth you need by laying the books out as shown in steps 1 through 3.

TO WRAP
Two books (each approx. 9 x 11 x ½ inches/23 x 28 x 1.5 cm)

CLOTH
Piece of cotton, 42 inches (105 cm) square

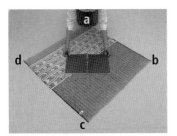

1. Spread cloth as a diamond, and place two books side by side in the center to gauge space needed.

2. Turn books over once each to left and right.

3. Cover left book with "b" and right with "d," tucking corners under.

4. Fold cloth and books in toward center.

5. Cross "a" and "c" vertically.

6. Still holding "a" and "c," fold the left book over the right so that the crossed material is on the inside, between the books.

7. Stand books up.

8. Twist "a" and "c," then tie ends using a square knot. (See page 23 for twisting instructions.)

Wrapping CDs

A traditional, sophisticated look for a simple gift. Try to envisage the finished look when positioning the CDs, and choose reasonably stiff cotton fabric.

TO WRAP
One or more CDs, small books, and so on.

CLOTH
Piece of cotton, 20 inches (50 cm) square

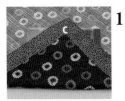

1. Spread cloth as a diamond. Place CDs on cloth, positioning them so "c" extends beyond the inner edge of the CD by about 1 inch (2.5 cm) to define the flap that spills over the edge of the finished wrap.

2. Carefully roll the CD top to bottom toward "a." Keep about 5 ½ inches (14 cm) between the bottom of the CDs and "a," with the left side of the CDs to the right of the vertical centerline.

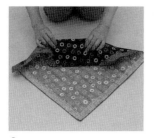

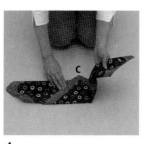

3. Cover CDs with "a" and roll.

4. Pull "c" over CDs so it extends beyond edge of CDs.

5. Bring "b" and "d" together and tie in a plain knot.

6. Angle ends of cloth in an interesting manner reminiscent of rabbit ears.

Rectangular Wrap

Fabric twisted tightly on top accentuates the oblong shape of the case, and doubles as a handle. Be careful where you place the case: get it wrong and the twisted end will be too short to tie. Twist the handle as tightly as possible before you tie the knot, since the cloth will inevitably loosen.

TO WRAP
Long, rectangular case or box (approx. 7 x 2 ½ x 1 inches/18 x 6.5 x 2.5 cm)

CLOTH
Piece of cotton, 20 inches (50 cm) square

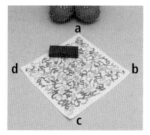

1. Spread cloth as a diamond and position box so that its bottom left corner is 6 inches (15 cm) from corner "a."

2. Place "a" over top and flip box over, . . .

3. . . . wrapping in the direction of "c."

4. Making sure the corners of the box are straight, twist "b" to form cord. (See page 23 for twisting instructions.)

5. Tie "b" and "d" at the edge of the box using a square knot.

Simple Flower Wrap

Fold a single piece of fabric and—presto!—you have a dainty flower that takes just moments to make. Be sure to master this basic floral wrapping technique before attempting more ambitious designs.

TO WRAP
Box (approx. 10 x 10 x 1 inches/25 x 25 x 2.5 cm)

CLOTH
Piece of rayon crepe, approx. 28 inches (70 cm) square

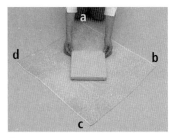

1. Spread cloth as a diamond and place box in center.

2. Bring "a" and "c" together . . .

3. . . . and pull tight.

4. While holding "a" and "c," cross "b" and "d" at the back and tie in a square knot at the front of "a" and "c."

5. Pull apart "a" and "c" to create an opening at center of knot.

6. Fold "a" over and insert in center of knot hole. Repeat with "c" to finish flower.

Carnation Wrap

Can you believe making this big, bold flower with your own hands is so easy? Selecting the right combination of colors and patterns for the two pieces of cloth makes all the difference to the finished item. Think of your favorite flowers as you choose. Naturally, with larger pieces of cloth (see page 19), this wrap will work beautifully for bigger packages, including circular boxes.

TO WRAP
Small book, box, or container (approx. 5 x 7 x 1 inches/12 x 17 x 2.5 cm)

CLOTH
Two pieces of rayon crepe, 18 inches (45 cm) square

1. Spread pieces of cloth on top of each other right-side down as a diamond, the outer cloth on the bottom, and that to form the flower on top.

2. Place gift in center.

3. Bring together all four corners of the top cloth.

4. Bring together "A" and "C" of the bottom piece, . . .

5. . . . bundling with corners of the top cloth.

6. Cross "B" and "D" round the back.

7. Tie in a square knot at the front.

8. Open six remaining corners out wide to form the petals of the flower, pulling to create opening in center of knot.

9. Fold four inner pieces in half inwards and push tips into knot hole to form flower.

10. Fold the two outer corners in half as well, and tuck under the flower petals. Tidy flower.

Falling Cherry Blossoms

The sight of falling petals inspired this design. The key is to aim for a natural look. The petals should look ruffled rather than orderly, as if they are about to fall. Avoid a finish that looks too tidy.

TO WRAP
Tin of tea (approx. 3 ½ x 3 ½ x 4 inches/9.5 x 9.5 x 10 cm)

CLOTH
Two pieces of silk crepe, approx. 18 inches (45 cm) square

1. Spread two pieces of fabric as a diamond, one on top of the other, and place tin in center.

2. Tie "b" and "d" of the top cloth in a half-knot.

3. Repeat for "a" and "c."

4. Tie "A" and "C" of the bottom cloth in a half-knot.

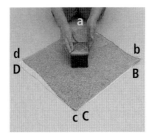

5. Gather up the six "petals."

6. While holding the petals, cross "B" and "D" in front of hand and . . .

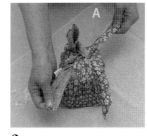

7. . . . tie at back using a square knot.

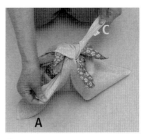

8. Pull out the fabric to form the six petals, and adjust for final look.

Ruby-Red Rose

Create a single perfect bloom for a special person on a special day. Everything is sure to come up roses with this graceful, gathered design using silky soft fabric.

TO WRAP
Plate (approx. 10 inches/25 cm in diameter)

CLOTH
Piece of rayon crepe, approx. 28 inches (70 cm) square

1. Lay out cloth as a diamond, and place plate in the center.

2. Bring "a" and "c" into center . . .

3. . . . and bundle together.

4. Cross "b" and "d" around the back of the bundled corners.

5. Tie at front using a square knot.

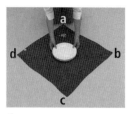

6. Pull "a" and "c" apart.

7. Make vertical pleats (see page 23) of around ½ inch (1 cm) in "a," and . . .

8. . . . wind around the back of center so pleat edges point up. Tuck in tip.

9. Repeat with "c" and wind in opposite direction.

10. Tie the tips of "a" and "d," and "c" and "b" in small, neat square knots to fasten. Tuck knots underneath the rose to conceal. Tidy rose.

Double Rose

This wrap offers twice the charm with a pair of delicate, dainty roses certain to raise a smile of delight. If possible use double-sided fabric to create blooms of different colors.

TO WRAP
Box (approx. 7 x 10 x 1 inches/18 x 25 x 2.5 cm)

CLOTH
Piece of rayon crepe, approx. 28 inches (70 cm) square

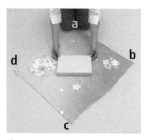

1. Spread the cloth as a diamond, and place box in center.

2. Bring "a" and "c" into center and bundle together.

3. Cross "b" and "d" around the back . . .

4. . . . and tie at front using a square knot.

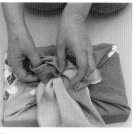

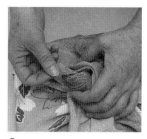

5. Pull "a" and "c" apart to open center.

6. Make vertical pleats of around ½ inch (1.5 cm) in "a."

7. Wind up around a thumb or finger to form rose.

8. Push tip through center of flower from bottom to top, allowing tip to peak out slightly from center. Repeat with "c" winding in the opposite direction to make second flower.

Flower and Butterfly

Choose a piece of cloth with a cheerful color combination to celebrate spring. If you are giving a gift in another season, select bright colors that suit the theme. The trick is to forget the details and just be bold!

TO WRAP
Box, CD, book, or other small item (approx. 4 ½ x 5 x 1 inches/12 x 13 x 2.5 cm)

CLOTH
Two pieces of rayon crepe, approx. 18 inches (45 cm) square

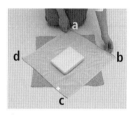

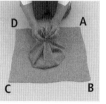

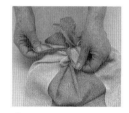

1. Spread cloth 1 as a square. Place cloth 2 on top as a diamond, then place the box in the center, its edges parallel to those of cloth 2.

2. Bring the four corners of cloth 2 together.

3. Tie "A" and "D" of cloth 1 around gathered corners in a square knot at the back.

4. Pull corners "b," "c," and "d" of cloth 2 outward and . . .

5. . . . insert tips in the center of the knot to fix in place.

6. Tie "B" and "C" of cloth 1 in a square knot and . . .

7. . . . fold corners under and tuck in to make butterfly.

8. Take "a" of cloth 2, fold into vertical pleats of about ½ inch (1 cm) right around and . . .

9. . . . tie a single, loose knot to form a rose in bloom.

10. Adjust wrapping as necessary to firm final shapes.

Basic Bottle Wrap

Perfect for wrapping a single bottle of wine, champagne, or saké. This design also features a convenient handle and adds a gracious touch to a thoughtful gift in a matter of seconds. Make fabric hug the lines of the bottle tightly for a neat, trim look. For a large 2-quart (1.8-liter) bottle of saké, use a 36-inch-square (90-cm) cloth.

TO WRAP
One bottle of wine (750 ml)

CLOTH
Piece of cotton, 28 inches (70 cm) square

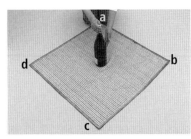

1. Spread cloth as a diamond and place bottle upright in center.

2. Tie "b" and "d" over the top of the bottle, using a square knot.

3. Turn wrap 90 degrees to the right. Pull "a" and "c" tight, then . . .

4. . . . cross them around the side closest to you and . . .

5. . . . tie them in a square knot. As you do so, bunch or fold in any excess fabric to bring out the silhouette of the bottle.

6. Half untie "b" and "d."

7. Twist the two free corners (see page 23), make a loop . . .

8. . . . and tie ends with a square knot to form the handle.

Twin Bottle Wrap

Simply lie the bottles down, roll them up and stand them up. The pattern of the cloth determines, the mood—festive, elegant, or romantic. A great way to show off your wrapping talent! To carry, loop your fingers under the knot.

TO WRAP
Two bottles of wine (750 ml each)

CLOTH
Piece of cotton, 36 inches (90 cm) square

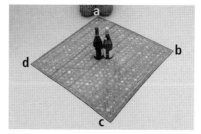

1. Stand bottles in center of cloth.

2. Lie bottles down bottom to bottom about 4 inches (10 cm) apart, pointing left and right.

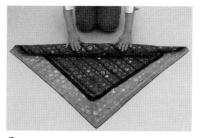

3. Bring corner "a" over bottles, then roll the bottles up in the cloth.

4. When there is no more cloth, grasp the bottles by their necks and stand them up.

5. Fasten them with a square knot, then tidy up the "bow" at the top.

All Dressed Up

Some enchanted evening, and in a stylish bow tie, your bottle will look almost as good as you. The trick is to gather any excess fabric close into the bottle for a sleek silhouette that highlights the bow.

TO WRAP
One bottle of wine (750 ml)

CLOTH
Piece of rayon (approx. 36 inches/90 cm) square

1. Spread cloth as a diamond, and place bottle about 2 inches (5 cm) forward of center.

2. Pull "c" over top of bottle, then cross "a" and "c" around bottle.

3. Tie in a square knot at back of bottle.

4. Lay the bottle down, with the knot facing up.

5. Pass "b" and "d" through knot from bottom to top, keeping each on its own side.

6. Pull any slack tight against bottle.

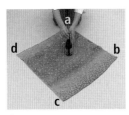

7. Stand bottle up. Twist "b" and "d."

8. Make a loop with "b" and pass the tip through the knot band at back, from top to bottom. Repeat with "d," but bring tip up from bottom to top.

9. Tie "b" and "d" into a small knot.

10. Open "a" and "c" and tuck tips under to form bow tie.

Kimono Beauty

Try wrapping an empty bottle and placing flowers or a small toy inside the folds of the kimono for a novel decoration.

TO WRAP
Small bottle of saké (720 ml)

CLOTH
Piece of polyester, approx. 18 inches (45 cm) square

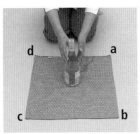

1. Spread cloth as a square, and place bottle upright so that the back edge of its base touches the centerline.

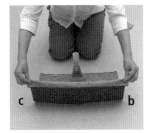

2. Fold side "b–c" outward 1 inch (2.5 cm).

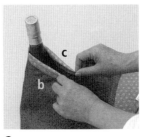

3. Arrange around neck of the bottle to look like the collar of a kimono, . . .

4. . . . pulling "c" over "b."

5. Fasten with a rubber band to secure.

6. Fold side "a–d" outward approx. 1 ½ inches (3–4 cm) to make an obi sash for the kimono.

7. Pull up to kimono waist, then pull ends around the back and tie a square knot.

CHOPSTICKS HOLDER

Great to present with sushi to guests. Dress chopsticks to complement your kimono-wrapped bottle. All you need to do is fold into a kimono style that can be used as a napkin when eating.

TO WRAP
Chopsticks (approx. 10 inches/25 cm long)

CLOTH
Fabric approx. 18 inches (45 cm) square

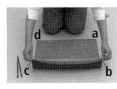

1. Spread cloth as a square, and fold side "b–c" outward about 1 inch (2.5 cm).

2. Fold "b" down.

3. Fold "c" over to make the collar of the kimono.

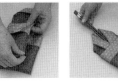

4. Fold side "a–d" up to make a kimono sash around 1 ½ inches (4 cm) wide, then bring up to bottom of kimono collar.

5. Tuck sides under to finish kimono.

6. Insert chopsticks.

Tipsy Lady

Perfect for whiskey and similar shorter, more compact bottles. Soft fabrics are ideal for this one: aim for the flowing lines of a trailing hem.

TO WRAP
A compact bottle of whiskey, brandy, etc. (approx. 640 ml)

CLOTH
Piece of rayon crepe, approx. 28 inches (70 cm) square

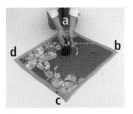

1. Spread cloth as a diamond and place bottle about 2 inches (5 cm) below the center.

2. Pass "c" over top of bottle and cross "a" and "c."

3. Tie in a half-knot at the shoulder of the bottle.

4. Twist "a" and "c" into "ropes" (see page 23), then make a loop and tie ends in a square knot.

5. Pass "b" through loop, and tie with "d" into a plain knot.

Perky Puppy Dog Wrap

Here is a frisky way to wrap a set of large cups or mugs as a gift, or even a single coffee mug for a colleague. The design incorporates the handle. For a larger mug, use a slightly larger square of cloth (20 inches/50 cm).

TO WRAP
Mug, 3–4 inches (8–10 cm) in diameter x 4 inches (10 cm) high

CLOTH
Piece of double-sided polyester, 18 inches (45 cm) square and 2 small buttons or beads

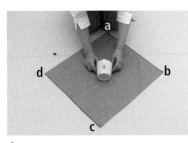

1. Spread cloth as a diamond. Lay mug on its side in the center of the cloth, with handle pointing up and base facing away from you.

2. Pass "b" and "d" in opposite directions through handle.

3. Pull corners gently but firmly.

4. Cross "b" and "d" over top of handle to cover and pass through once more. Pull out. These one the ears.

5. Pass "a" and "c" between ears and tie in a half-knot on top over handle.

6. Twist, make a loop, and tie ends using a square knot. Press down.

7. Place cup upright and attach eyes. Adjust face and ears.

Cute Kitty Bowl Wrap

A set of small bowls makes the perfect house-warming gift. They could be petite soup bowls or desert dishes. This wrap integrates form with function, relying on the bowl's basic shape to form the cat's face. For larger bowls, use larger cloths.

TO WRAP
Small bowl 3–4 inches (8–10 cm) in diameter and 2 buttons or beads.

CLOTH
Piece of cotton, 20 inches (50 cm) square

1. Spread cloth out as a square, and place bowl in center.

2. Tie "a" and "d" in a half-knot on top of bowl.

3. Pass "b" over knot toward bottom right corner. Pass "c" over "b" toward bottom left corner.

4. Tie "a" and "d" together in a square knot over "b" and "c."

5. Turn bowl over and attach eyes with glue or thread. Adjust ears and face to finish.

Wreath #1

Wreaths can add a decorative touch to your home for any season. Whether its spring, summer, fall, or winter, you can create your own wreaths by choosing appropriate colors and a small seasonal element. Textiles make for a look that is both cozy and stylish: all it takes is a little imagination.

TO WRAP
Craft wire (approx. 22 inches/55 cm long, 1/8 inch/ 5 mm thick)

CLOTH
Piece of fabric, approx. 20 inches (50 cm) square

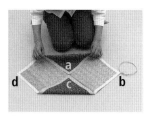

1. Use craft wire to make a ring around 5 inches (13 cm) in diameter. Spread cloth as a diamond. Fold cloth in eighths lengthwise by bringing "a" and "c" into the center, then bringing the edges at "a" and "c" into the center, and folding again, making the cloth 1/8 of its original width.

2. Fold in half.

3. Hold one end of cloth above wire ring.

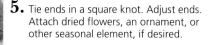

4. Wind cloth around wire.

5. Tie ends in a square knot. Adjust ends. Attach dried flowers, an ornament, or other seasonal element, if desired.

NOTE: For large wreath, use a 28-inch-square (70-cm) piece of fabric and a 24-inch (60-cm) length of wire.

Wreath #2

When you make a wreath with two pieces of cloth, the possibilities for creativity multiply. Not only can you add a second solid tone, but a long draping tail, which brings an unexpected elegance to the finished piece.

TO WRAP
Craft wire (approx. 24 inches/60 cm long, 1/8 inch/ 5 mm thick)

CLOTH
Two pieces of fabric, approx. 20 inches (50 cm) square

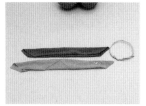

1. Use craft wire to make a ring around 7 inches (18 cm) in diameter. Fold both cloths up as in previous steps 1 and 2.

2. Hold one end of cloth above wire ring.

3. Wind first cloth halfway around the ring.

4. Pull "tail" out.

5. Wind second cloth around the other half.

6. Tie tops of the cloths together in a square knot.

7. Wind the tail end of one cloth around the other, then tie in a plain knot.

INTERIOR WRAPS FOR THE HOME

A single piece of fabric can radically change the appearance of a room. It is amazing how wrapping and casually positioning an object can add a whole new dimension to your interiors. Wrap unwanted items to give them a new lease on life as fixtures and fittings, or to rediscover their original charm. Put your skill with textiles to work, and add color and intrigue to your surroundings.

Wrapped Basket

Transform a spare basket or container into a stylish container with a handle. A handy wrapping style with a multitude of uses in everyday living, use this design for containers of any shape or size. Note the dimensions of the cloth and basket carefully. If the cloth is too big, twist both sides of the handle tighter to take in the excess before tying the final knot. If the cloth is small, don't bother twisting the handle at all. The perfect container for fruit, cookies, or candy.

TO WRAP
Basket or other container around 12 inches (30 cm) in diameter and 4 inches (10 cm) high

CLOTH
Piece of cotton, 42 inches (105 cm) square

1. Spread cloth as a diamond and place basket in center.

2. Place "a" over basket, and push some cloth into basket to cover center.

3. From the opposite direction, repeat with "c."

4. Tie single knots at the base of "b" and "d" so that they stand up at the basket edges.

5. Twist "b" and "d" (see page 23).

6. Tie in a square knot at top.

Wrapped Baskets

■ VARIATION 1

Use these methods for a square box, or perhaps a round basket. Or use them to wrap any container, of any shape or size, made from any material. Each of these variations shares its initial steps with the previous wrap. Enjoy creating your own styles for your breakfast table or to set around the house as containers for decorative or useful items.

TO WRAP
Tin, box, or other container (approx. 8 ½ x 3 x 2 ½ inches/22 x 8.5 x 6 cm)

CLOTH
Piece of cotton, 20 inches (50 cm) square

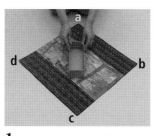

1. Spread cloth as a diamond and place container in center.

2. Place "a" over container, and pull tight to base.

3. Repeat with "c."

4. Tie single knots at the base of "b" and "d" so that they stand up at the container's edge.

5. Tie "b" and "d" in a square knot.

■ VARIATION 2

Use this to make a container for keys, small change, or other little items.

TO WRAP
Plastic box, 6 x 4 x 2 inches (15 x 10 x 5 cm)

CLOTH
Piece of cotton, 20 inches (50 cm) square

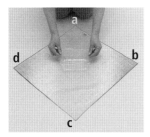

1. Spread cloth as a diamond and place box in the center.

2. Place "a" over box and press to fit bottom.

3. Repeat with "c."

4. Tie "b" and "d" in a single knot at edges of box so that they sit up straight.

Graceful Greenery

Note the lovely frill at the front of this plant container, with the added charm of beautiful fabric. Use this design to wrap anything from a potted plant to bowls of various sizes. Just remember to choose a cloth of generous dimensions.

TO WRAP
Potted plant (approx. 8 inches/20 cm in diameter x 2 ¾ inches/7 cm high)

CLOTH
Piece of rayon crepe, approx. 28 inches (70 cm) square

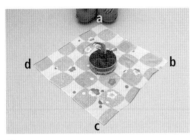

1. Spread cloth as a diamond, and place pot in the center.

2. Fold "b" toward the center and slip under the pot. The height of the remaining cloth should reach 1 inch (2.5 cm) higher than the height of the lip. Adjust "b" as necessary.

3. Turn planter 180° degrees. Repeat the process with "d," this time making the cloth only slightly higher than the lip of the container.

4. Rotate planter ninety degrees to bring "b" closer to you. Make vertical pleats around 1 ½ inches (3 cm) wide in the folded section of "b."

5. Holding the pleats in place, gather "a" up tight against the back of the pleats.

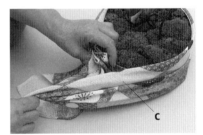

6. Pull "c" around pot to back of pleats.

7. Pull up pleats, then tie "a" and "c" in a square knot over them.

Elegant Planter

Is this the latest trend in vases? No, just two empty cans and a cloth transformed into an elegant planter. This design calls for firm, well-balanced knots. Give the knot in the middle a little more fabric (around 5 ½ inches/14 cm for one end, 2 inches/5 cm for the other), while the tails of the knots on either side should be the same length. Use cans of the same size.

TO WRAP
Two empty cans (approx. 4 ½ inches/11.5 cm in diameter x 6 inches/15 cm high)

CLOTH
Piece of rayon crepe, approx. 28 inches (70 cm) square

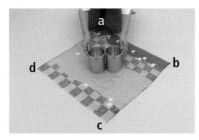

1. Spread cloth as a diamond, and place cans side by side in center.

2. Bring "a" and "c" together.

3. Tie in a plain knot at the front, in the gap between the cans.

4. Gather corner "b" and pull tight, keeping the top of the can open.

5. Tie a single knot in "b." Repeat previous step for "d" and tie single knot. Adjust knots on both sides of the planter for symmetry, as well as the material around the top edges of the cans.

Decorative Cushion Wrap

An ingenious way to transform a battered old cushion into a fresh item for any room in the house. Try wrapping cushions with a variety of textiles to highlight the mood in different rooms, or to complement the season. This wrap uses two pieces of fabric, one for the basic wrap and the other for effect, creating a loose yet intriguing finish.

TO WRAP
Cushion (approx. 16 x 16 x 5 inches/40 x 40 x 13 cm)

CLOTH
Two pieces of fabric, 28 inches (70 cm) square

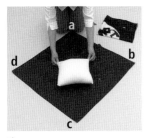

1. Spread cloth as a diamond, and place cushion above the horizontal line running from "b" to "d."

2. Tie "a" and "c" in a square knot at the back edge of the cushion.

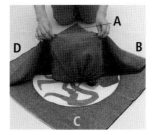

3. Spread other piece of cloth as a diamond, and stand up pillow in the center with the knot down.

4. Tie "A" and "C" in a square knot.

5. Tie "b" and "B", then "d" and "D" in plain knots.

Tissue-Box Cover

This is the simplest wrap in the book. Two knots, a quick adjustment to the fabric and you have a new decorative element for your room. Choose a fabric to match or accent the surroundings. Don't worry if your tissue box is of slightly different dimensions. The versatility of cloth makes it easy: simply use a larger or smaller piece of cloth if necessary.

TO WRAP
Tissue box (approx. 9½ x 5 x 3½ inches/24 x 13 x 9 cm)

CLOTH
Piece of cotton, 20 inches (50 cm) square

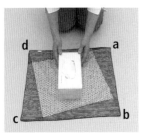

1. Spread cloth out as a square and place tissue box in the center.

2. Tie "a" and "d" in a firm square knot, pulling tight to the edge of the box.

3. Repeat for "c" and "b."

4. Finish each side by tucking any excess fabric under knot to tidy corners. Tidy opening for tissues.

Quick Wrapping for Large Flat Objects

Use this wrapping technique to transport large flat objects by yourself with ease, or to wrap a framed poster. Designers and artists will find this method perfect for carting around materials.

TO WRAP
Panel (approx. 24 x 40 x 1 inches/60 x 100 x 2.5 cm)

CLOTH
Piece of cotton, approx. 80 inches (200 cm) square

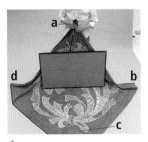

1. Spread cloth as a diamond, and place board upright in center, supporting it with "a."

2. Tie "a" and "c" in a half-knot on top of board.

3. Make a loop (twisting optional; see page 23) and tie at top in a square knot.

4. Bring "b" into the center. Repeat for "d."

5. Tie "b" and "d" firmly in a square knot.

Tube Wrap

This is one everybody should know: carry a tube or other long object this way once and you'll wonder how you ever managed before. Ideal for transporting or storing plans or blueprints, and a great way to wrap a special poster for a friend.

TO WRAP
Tube or cylindrical object (approx. 30 inches long x 2 ½ inches in diameter/75 cm x 6.5 cm)

CLOTH
Piece of cotton, 48 inches (120 cm) square

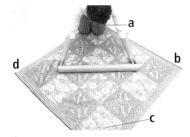

1. Spread cloth as a diamond, and place tube in the center.

2. Bring "a" and "c" into the center . . .

3. . . . and cross "a" toward "b," and "c" toward "d."

4. Cross "a" and "b," pulling to left end of the tube.

5. Wrap "b" once around the body of tube . . .

6. . . . then tie "a" and "b" into a square knot. Repeat with "c" and "d."

Backpack

Use this backpack to carry things, or hang it on a chair as a receptacle. This bag is not only handy, but an asset to any interior if a decorative fabric is selected. Choose a bright, cheery color combination, and make sure the knots connecting straps and bag are firm.

CLOTH
Two pieces of rayon crepe, approx. 28 inches (70 cm) square

1. Use one cloth for the strap. Spread cloth as a diamond. Fold "a" and "c" to the center in 2 to 3 inch (5 to 8 cm) bands until cloth has been folded into eighths.

2. Fold in half lengthwise.

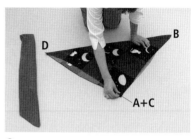

3. Use the second cloth to make the bag. Spread cloth as a diamond. Fold "A" to "C."

4. Tie "A" and "C" in a half-knot.

5. Place center of strap on top of half knot.

6. Tie square knot with "A" and "C" to attach strap to bag.

7. Tie strap end "b" and bag corner "B" in a square knot. Repeat for "d" and "D."

Instant Bag

A versatile addition to any kitchen or living room to store magazines and knicknacks, this bag is also ideal for gardening or handcrafts. A few knots are all it takes to make a roomy bag with a generous, accessible opening. Make sure to pull at least 2 inches (5 cm) of fabric out of the top knot. The knots at the left and right edges should be around one-third of the way up either side. Too low, and the contents of the bag will spill out.

CLOTH
Piece of cotton, 42 inches (105 cm) square

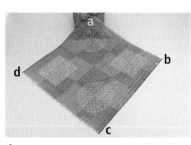

1. Spread cloth as a diamond.

2. Tie "a" and "c" using a square knot to form the top of the bag.

3. Pull "b" straight out and tie it into a single large, sturdy knot about one-third the way up the side of the bag.

4. Repeat for "d."

Towel Hanger

As simple as the tissue-box wrap, and as attractive: simply fold the fabric into a narrow strip, make a loop and tie with a square knot. Thick fabric will not require a core for support, but if using a thinner fabric, wrap it loosely around craft or ordinary wire, or a coat hanger, so that the loop keeps its shape.

CLOTH
Piece of cotton, 20 inches (50 cm) square

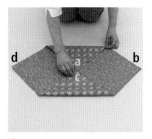

1. Spread cloth as a diamond, and fold "a" and "c" into center.

2. Fold "a" and "c" edges into center.

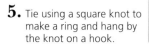

3. Fold in half.

4. Twist cloth into a "rope."

5. Tie using a square knot to make a ring and hang by the knot on a hook.

Coathanger Cover

This wrap transforms an ordinary coathanger into a thing of beauty. Handy for keeping items such as delicate silk blouses firmly on the hanger. Even the most inexpensive fabric will add a touch of class in the right setting.

TO WRAP
Wire coathanger

CLOTH
Two pieces of polyster, approx. 28 inches (70 cm) square

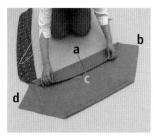

1. Spread out the first cloth as a diamond. Fold cloth in eighths lengthwise by bringing "a" and "c" into the center, then bringing the edge at "a" and "c" into the center.

2. Repeat with second cloth.

3. Lay ends of cloth over top of hanger.

4. Fasten both cloths to top of hanger using a square knot.

5. Wind cloth 1 around hanger to halfway point.

6. Cover remaining half with cloth 2.

7. Tie ends of cloths at bottom in a half-knot.

8. Twist remaining fabric to make a loop and tie ends in a square knot. The loop can be used to hang items such as neckties and scarves.

9. Optional: Create a small opening in top knot. Insert corners of cloth into center to make a butterfly.

Wastepaper Receptacle

Wrap a plain wastepaper basket with an attractive piece of fabric and suddenly a distracting eyesore becomes a decorative element for your room. This will work for any largish receptacle, even a cardboard box. Fabric of any quality may be used; the key is to knot it firmly at the corners of the box.

TO WRAP
Wastepaper receptacle approx. 9 inches (23 cm) in diameter x 12 inches (30 cm) high

CLOTH
Piece of cotton, 36 inches (90 cm) square

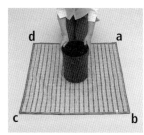

1. Spread cloth as a square, and place receptacle in the center.

2. Tie "a" and "b" together at edge of wastepaper basket using a square knot.

3. Repeat for "c" and "d" on the opposite side.

4. Tuck surplus fabric under both knots.

Table Setting

Whether an intimate dinner for two or a small gathering of friends, setting the scene with wrapped wine and a bouquet of flowers adds a warm, homemade touch to the event.

Wrapping Wine

Sure to attract compliments at any gathering or as a gift, this wrapping is one party trick worth remembering! The key is to make big, generous pleats, then open them right out at the back, and tidy to finish.

TO WRAP
Bottle of wine (750 ml)

CLOTH
Piece of polyester, approx. 28 inches (70 cm) square

1. Spread cloth as a diamond and stand bottle in center.

2. Fold "c" into center, adjusting until the folded section of cloth, when raised, is the same height as the bottle.

3. Raise and compare folded section to bottle as often as necessary.

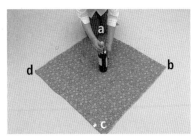

4. Make vertical pleats (see page 22) about 1 inch (3 cm) wide in the folded section.

5. Bring up pleats to the top of the bottle, and fasten to the neck with a rubber band. Repeat steps 2 through 5 for "a."

6. Open out "b" and "d" to left and right.

7. Cross over behind bottle, and bring round to the front.

8. Lie bottle down and tie "b" and "d" in front, where the rubber band is, using a square knot.

9. Stand bottle up. Remove rubber band, and spread pleats out to right and left.

Bouquet

Wrapping flowers in fabric highlights their beauty to great effect. The key is to choose a colored cloth that complements the flowers and does not detract from their natural beauty. Try working with colored paper once in a while as an alternative.

TO WRAP
Bouquet around 18 inches (45 cm) long

CLOTH
One piece of polyester, approx. 28 inches (70 cm) square

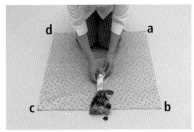

1. Spread cloth as a square and position bouquet slightly above center so flowers protrude beyond the far edge.

2. Fold "b" and "c" under, then . . .

3. . . . tie "b" and "c" in a square knot over the flowers.

4. Fold side "a–d" up, then turn edge outward to form a 1 ½ inch (4 cm) band of cloth, adjusting band to suit the size of the bouquet, if necessary.

5. Tuck "a" and "d" under the bouquet and bring each corner out the opposite side.

6. Tie "a" and "d" on top in a square knot.

HISTORY

In Japan, wrapping is an activity of great importance. Whether for preserving, storing, tidying, or gift giving, it is an integral part of daily life. The custom of gift giving led, over several centuries, to the emergence of many wrapping techniques.

Generally speaking, gifts are given as a way of conveying congratulations or gratitude, as a welcome, or to say "Well done!" or "Thank you!" When giving gifts to celebrate major rites of passage such as marriage and the birth of children, the Japanese traditionally use square pieces of cloth known as *furoshiki* or *fukusa* (crepe wrappers). The gift is wrapped in a furoshiki or fukusa of suitable design for the purpose, such as a lucky pattern, and delivered in person to the recipient's home.

People in Japan avoid giving cash or goods unwrapped. This idea has its origins in a courtesy that became everyday etiquette in samurai households during the Kamakura (1185–1333) and Muromachi periods (1333–1568). Strict rules for wrapping were also established at this time. The late Iwao Nukada (1911–1993), who studied wrapping and knotting techniques, noted that "the way things were wrapped reflected the value of the contents, and the value of the person bringing the gift" (*Tsutsumi*, 1997). Presenting something unwrapped was deemed a breech of etiquette, and lowered the status of the giver in the eyes of the recipient.

■ ■ ■

The prototype of the furoshiki, the most common cloth used in Japan for gift wrapping, is the *hokei-fuhaku* (literally, "square fabric") like that found in the Shosoin Treasure House. Dating back to the Nara period (eighth century), the hokei-fuhaku is said to have been used for wrapping items such as the stoles of Buddhist priests and the costumes of minstrels. At that time, wrapping cloths were known as *tsutsumi* (wrapping) or *hirazutsumi* (flat wrapping). The tenth-century work *Wamyorui Josho*, written by Minamoto no Shitago (911–83), mentions the cloth and refers to it as *koromo-tsutsumi* (garment wrapping). The twelfth-century illustrated fan known as *Senmen Koshakyo Shitae*, meanwhile, depicts a woman carrying a furoshiki-wrapped bundle on her head, while in the treatise on costume, the *Masasuke Shozokusho* (1343), "a flat wrapping" cloth is discussed.

Furoshiki is written with the characters for *furo* (bath; 風呂) and *shiki* (from the verb "to lay"; 敷). How did cloth and the bath first become associated? In the Muromachi period, the shogun Ashikaga Yoshimitsu (1358–1408) built a large bathhouse in the capital, which he used to entertain military commanders from all over the land. It is said that when using the baths, the visiting commanders wrapped their garments in fukusa decorated with their family crest, to make it easy to distinguish their own clothing.

Wrapping cloths became known as furoshiki from the middle of the Edo period (1603–1868), the name spreading from the bathhouses that became a common sight in the capital at this time. The novelist Nanrei Tada claims in the posthumous *Nanrei Iko* (1757) that "the furoshiki was named after what was laid on the floor when getting out of the bath," while in the *Kottoshu* (1808), a book on antiques by artist and writer Kyoden Santo, it is suggested that the furoshiki "was a piece of cloth for laying down at the bath, and even though it is now used to wrap things, the bath [furo] name remains."

It is around this time that the use of cotton, introduced from overseas, began in Japan on a large scale, bringing with it the rapid proliferation of furoshiki, which came to be used not only for the bath, but as a means of bundling clothing in a knotted cloth for easy carrying. Also around this time, Japan's political situation stabilized and the lives of ordinary people took on a new vitality, with far broader horizons. Traveling for pleasure and itinerant peddling became common pursuits, and the furoshiki played a vital role in transporting goods for sale, and belongings when traveling.

Around 1900, advances in textile production, such as automated looms from overseas, led to a plethora of new fabrics and even greater use of furoshiki. In the earlier Edo period, samurai and wealthy merchant families would assemble a trousseau of "bridal furoshiki" of different sizes bearing the family crest and lucky designs for their daughters on marriage. However, with the advent of mass-produced furoshiki, this custom became established among ordinary working-class people as well. Indigo dyers known as *konya* could be found all over Japan, dyeing these bridal furoshiki. Once married, daughters would use the cloths for storage and to carry things, and the smaller ones to wrap gifts.

This is also when furoshiki were widely adopted for gift presentation. It became the custom to adorn a gift with a strip of *noshi* paper as a mark of respect or congratulations, wrap it in a furoshiki, and on arrival at the recipient's home, say one's piece, unwrap the furoshiki in front of them and present the gift.

The powerful influence of American culture following the post–World War II occupation of Japan by U.S. armed forces rapidly transformed the traditional Japanese way of life and values, including the custom of bridal furoshiki, which fell into decline. The furoshiki as a means of transporting things gave way to bags made of various materials including paper, and with the spread of plastic bags following the appearance of supermarkets across Japan in the

1970s, the furoshiki faded from view, while as a means of storage it was replaced by alternatives such as plastic boxes. It is around this time also that having gifts sent to the recipient's home directly by the department store became common practice. Beginning in 1980, the custom of wrapping a gift in a furoshiki, taking it to the recipient's home, and presenting it in person fell into decline.

However, when Japan's speculative boom, dubbed the "bubble economy," ended around 1990, people gradually began to rethink the lifestyle of mass consumption and mass disposal that had been spawned by the bubble. The furoshiki, part of everyday Japanese life since ancient times, can be used over and over again and generates no waste. Once again it was in the spotlight, this time as a way of helping to save the environment.

■ ■ ■

It is in light of these developments that I began to see the furoshiki, with its long history rooted in the everyday culture of Japan, as deserving of a higher place in the modern world. Seeking ways to utilize furoshiki in our daily lives, one idea I had was to use it as gift wrapping. Until now, the usual practice in Japan has been to wrap a gift in a furoshiki, then unwrap it and give the recipient just the gift. My suggestion is to give the furoshiki, or piece of fabric, as part of the gift. By wrapping a gift in a piece of carefully selected fabric, the giver can express the purpose of the gift, echo the spirit of the season, or show their feelings for the recipient. And handing it over in person is sure to bring the latter even greater joy.

The receipient can then reuse the cloth, and so the cycle continues: a piece of cloth used over and over again, a cultural and emotional connection from one person to the next.

For my part, I sincerely hope that this new concept of fun, environment-friendly textile gift wrapping will take root in many countries, and in turn become a new element of the act of gift giving as developed by the Japanese many generations ago.

A bridal furoshiki with a *noshi* motif from the Meiji period (1868–1912).

TRADITIONAL JAPANESE FUROSHIKI

Long Life and Chrysanthemums
Furoshiki with a "good fortune" design featuring the two characters used to celebrate long life, teamed with a sprinkling of chrysanthemums, symbols of longevity. The family crest at bottom left is a Chinese bellflower. (Cotton *tsutsugaki* [batik using rice paste], approx. 26½ x 28 inches/66 x 70 cm)

Treasure Trove
Furoshiki designed to bring happiness and prosperity. The design encompasses an array of treasures including a magic cloak that renders the wearer invisible, a purse, a clove motif, jewels, a cornucopia, and the "seven treasures." (Cotton *tsutsugaki*, approx. 26½ x 30½ inches/66 x 76 cm)

Carp Swimming up Waterfall
Depicting an intrepid carp that has swum up the shallow rapids at the upper reaches of the Yellow River and turned into a dragon, this furoshiki may have been made to celebrate the birth of a boy, as the carp traditionally symbolizes worldly success. (Cotton *tsutsugaki*, approx. 38½ x 45 inches/96 x 113 cm)

Shellfish Bucket Pattern
Clam shells used in a traditional Japanese game only fit their corresponding shell, making them a potent symbol of marital harmony. In wealthy families, brides once took lacquered wooden buckets of these shells to their new home as part of their trousseau, a custom incorporated into the design of this furoshiki. (Cotton *tsutsugaki*, approx. 41 x 44 inches/103 x 110 cm)

Sho-Chiku-Bai
The Okinawan dyeing technique of *bingata* has been employed to excellent effect here to depict the pine (*sho*), which remains green through even the coldest winter; bamboo (*chiku*), which springs back even when bowed by snow; and the plum tree (*bai*), which blossoms despite the cold, in a good-fortune pattern known as *saikan-sanyu*, literally "three friends in the cold," a reference to the priceless nature of friends that stand by us through everything. (Linen *bingata*, approx. 44 x 46 inches/110 x 115 cm)

Abundant Harvest
Furoshiki featuring a pair of cranes, most likely representing husband and wife, and heavily laden stalks of rice, expressing the desire not only for an abundant grain harvest, but also for marital harmony and many children. (Cotton *tsutsugaki*, 40 x 44 inches/100 x 110 cm)

Quilted Furoshiki
Furoshiki with quilted, reinforced corners and the Kanemasa shop name. Probably from the later Edo period. (Quilted cotton *tsutsugaki*, 51 x 57½ inches/128 x 144 cm)

Hawk and Stormy Seas
A hawk glides above the sea in stately splendor, unperturbed by the treacherous waves (depicted in stylized form) sending up clouds of spray. A heroic scene symbolizing the hope that a boy will have valor. (Cotton *tsutsugaki*, approx. 41 x 46 inches/103 x 115 cm)

Okina
"Okina" is a Noh play performed at festivities and other sacred rituals. A celebratory furoshiki featuring the mask worn by Okina as he dances, praying for peace and tranquility under the heavens, and the box used to contain that mask, as well as the nobleman's headwear, bell, and fan belonging to the character Sanbaso. (Cotton *tsutsugaki*, approx. 43 x 43 inches/108 x 108 cm)

Long Life and Chrysanthemums

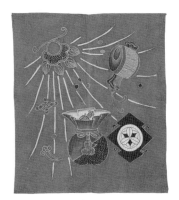

Treasure Trove

Carp Swimming up Waterfall

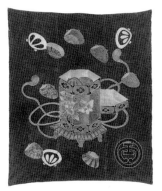

Shellfish Bucket Pattern

Sho-Chiku-Bai

Abundant Harvest

Quilted Furoshiki

Hawk and Stormy Seas

Okina

From the Mitsuo Toyoda collection

■協力　中山道広重美術館　Hiroshige Museum of Art, Ena
　　　（p. 90 渓斎英泉「木曽街道　蕨之驛　戸田川渡場」）

　　　慶應義塾　Keio University
　　　（p. 92 右　窪 俊満「菜の花道」）

　　　豊田満夫　Mitsuo Toyoda
　　　（p. 95　ふろしきコレクション）

■撮影協力　Neutral
　　　　　GOSPEL

（英文版）ふろしきラッピング
Gift Wrapping with Textiles

2005年11月　第 1 刷発行
2009年 2 月　第 4 刷発行

著　者　　森田知都子
撮　影　　山形 秀一
翻　訳　　カースティン・マカイヴァー
発行者　　富田　充
発行所　　講談社インターナショナル株式会社
　　　　　〒112-8652 東京都文京区音羽 1-17-14
　　　　　電話　03-3944-6493（編集部）
　　　　　　　　03-3944-6492（営業部・業務部）
　　　　　ホームページ　www.kodansha-intl.com
印刷・製本所　　大日本印刷株式会社